# EXTREME
## COMMITMENT

# RON LUCE

# IF YOUR NAME'S NOT

## ————————————————————,

# GET YOUR HANDS
# OFF ME!

NexGen® is an imprint of
Cook Communications Ministries, Colorado Springs, CO 80918
Cook Communications, Paris, Ontario
Kingsway Communications, Eastbourne, England

OVER THE EDGE: EXTREME COMMITMENT
© Copyright 2006 by Ron Luce
Ron Luce is the founder and president of Teen Mania Ministries.

First printing 2006
Printed in South Korea
                    1 2 3 4 5 6 7 8 9 10  Printing/Year  11 10 09 08 07 06
Cover Design: BMB Design
Interior Design: Helen Harrison (Ya-Ye Design)
Cover Photo: istockphoto

Full source documentation for statistical information can be found in the Rise Up:
Basic Training for Warriors Leader's Guide.

ISBN: 0-78144-385-7

**SO YOU'VE EXPERIENCED RISE UP: BASIC TRAINING FOR WARRIORS.** Maybe your youth group did it over one pressure cooker of a weekend. Or maybe you went through it week by week, letting each session sink in. Did it wring you out and hang you up to dry? Are you still feeling damp? Well, guess what—*we're not through with you yet.*

No matter what your personal basic training looked like, it takes time to turn life-changing decisions into daily commitments and permanent habits. So brace yourself—it's time for Round 2 with **OVER THE EDGE: EXTREME COMMITMENT.**

# BASIC TRAINING FOR WARRIORS: REVISITED

Before you dive *Over the Edge*, let's do a quick review of the basic training experience.

## SESSION 1: LIGHTING THE DARKNESS

At the very beginning you were reminded of your sin nature—that struggle you feel when you're tempted. You chose to turn and run to God and away from that sin nature. You repented and put your foot down to the sins that had taken hold of your life. You were cleansed by the blood of Jesus.

## SESSION 2: WHO ARE YOU?

In the second session you learned to see yourself and others through God's eyes. You learned how to value yourself because of how God sees you, not how the world sees you.

## SESSION 3: THE THINGS YOU COULDN'T SAY "NO" TO

During this session you faced the things that have plagued you for a long time—addictive sins. You chose to plant your roots in the Word, not the world. You left those addictions at the foot of the cross and were set free. You will continue to find that freedom as you dig into God's Word and discover new strength.

## SESSION 4: YOUR INNER CIRCLE

During Session Four you took a hard look at your friendships. You made some adjustments when you realized some of those friendships were unhealthy. You identified both an accountability partner and an advisor who will be honest with you and encourage you in your walk with God.

Then you did something that will forever change your family: You released all unforgiveness toward your family. You forgave your parents. You committed to going home and making things right with them. You also forgave members of the youth group who had hurt you.

## SESSION FIVE: INSIGNIFICANT OTHERS

In this session you broke off soul ties from past relationships and allowed God to make you whole again, taking back pieces of yourself you had given away. You forgave those who had hurt you in past relationships, releasing that bitterness forever. You were challenged to "crush the crush," committing at least one year to running after God instead of a guy or girl.

## SESSION SIX: ALL DRESSED UP AND NOWHERE TO GO

In Session Six, you caught a glimpse of the massive army you're a part of. You now know that God has an incredible purpose for your life. He is calling you to reach the world for Him. You answered that call. You're ready for battle.

## SESSION SEVEN: FIELD ASSIGNMENT

You were challenged to take the lessons of *Basic Training for Warriors* and do something about them! Will your heart be like the shallow soil that could not support the seeds trying take root in it—or will your heart become rich, spiritual soil that God can use to produce an amazing harvest for His glory?

# HOW TO USE OVER THE EDGE

## HOW IT WORKS

*Over the Edge: Extreme Commitment* contains seven chapters; you'll be going through one chapter a week. Each chapter revisits one session from *Rise Up: Basic Training for Warriors* and includes five days' worth of personal Bible studies and log entries. Each week also begins with a memory verse. Make it a point to look at this verse every day. This is your chance to truly etch God's Word on your heart!

You'll want to have your Bible with you as you go through each day's study. You get to dig into the Word every day and discover the truth that God has in store for you. This process will help you take the lessons of *Rise Up: Basic Training for Warriors* to a deeper level.

## "NOTES" PAGES

At the end of each week of log entries, you'll find a couple of open pages. These are "extras" for you to use when you need more space to write or to express your thoughts through drawings and doodles. Express yourself!

## YOUR EXTREME COMMITMENT PARTNER

You know that accountability partner you chose in Session Four? This person is going to be your *Extreme Commitment* partner, too. You'll continue to "check in" with your partner on a regular basis, letting him or her know how you're doing with the process. How is God speaking to you? What areas are the toughest for you to deal with? How can your partner help you stay on track? Think about it.

If your *Extreme Commitment* partner is someone from the youth group, you two can navigate this experience together!

## YOUR ACCOUNTABILITY ADVISOR

During Session Four you also chose an accountability advisor. Maybe you asked your youth leader or another adult in the church to be this person for you. He or she will commit to walk with you through this process for the next several weeks.

If you find yourself struggling with one of the issues raised in *Basic Training for Warriors,* your advisor can guide you through the difficulties. Remember to give them a call; let them know what's up in your life.

## STUCK?

Falling behind on your log entries? Feeling like you bit off more than you can chew? Don't give up! *Over the Edge: Extreme Commitment* does call for a commitment from you, but this isn't about dotting every "i" and crossing every "t." This is about making a decision to follow Christ wholeheartedly—and then learning how to do that. Some parts of the process may be downright painful. Don't be afraid of that—God is healing you and giving you a wonderful opportunity to go deep with Him! Stick with it. You won't regret it.

**EACH OF US** may be sure that, if God sends us over rocky paths, He will provide us with sturdy shoes. He will never send us on any journey without equipping us well.

Alexander MacLaren

**THE FIRST SESSION OF BASIC TRAINING** aimed a pretty bright light onto the shadowy places in your life. You learned about your sin nature and the battle that rages for your heart and mind every day. You also got a strong reminder that sin is repulsive.

But wait—you learned some other things, too. **YOU CAN RUN TO GOD WHEN SIN COMES KNOCKING AT YOUR DOOR.** After all, He sent Jesus Christ—His own Son—to pay the price for your sins. All of them.

Even though you **BELONG TO GOD,** the enemy of your soul would still love to keep your loyalty divided. So he finds out what your weaknesses are, and **PUSHES THOSE BUTTONS** as often as possible.

It's easy to repent during the intensity of a retreat weekend and say, "I'll never do that again." But you're back in the "real world" now, and **EVERY DAY YOU WILL HAVE TO MAKE CHOICES.** God always provides a way to escape temptation. Will you hang around and give it another shot at you?

**OR WILL YOU RUN?**

**MEMORIZE . . .**

Therefore, since we are surrounded
by such a great cloud of witnesses, let
us throw off everything that hinders
and the sin that so easily entangles, and let us run with perseverance the race marked out for us.

—Hebrews 12:1

**WRITE GOD'S WORD** on your heart this week by memorizing Hebrews 12:1.

**REPEAT THIS VERSE** every day until it becomes a part of you. You can use these pages to practice memorizing Hebrews 12:1. Write it out or draw it in doodle form.

**IT HAPPENS SO REGULARLY** that it's predictable. The moment I decide to do good, sin is there to trip me up. I truly delight in God's commands, but it's pretty obvious that not all of me joins in that delight. Parts of me covertly rebel, and just when I least expect it, they take charge.

**I'VE TRIED EVERYTHING** and nothing helps. I'm at the end of my rope. Is there no one who can do anything for me? Isn't that the real question?

The answer, thank God, is that **JESUS CHRIST CAN AND DOES.** He acted to set things right in this life of contradictions where I want to serve God with all my heart and mind, but am pulled by the influence of sin to do something totally different.
—**Romans 7:21–25 (The Message)**

**DURING YOUR BASIC TRAINING** experience, your youth group engaged in a ferocious tug-of-war. That battle represented our struggles with sin. Remember the drawing of the rope in your Student Training Manual? Remember how easy it is to give in to temptation?

Your student manual had you list some things that tend to pull you away from God and toward your sin nature. Think back to that exercise and to the sins you named.

# INSPECTION

Do any of the sins on that list still give you a hard time? If so, which ones?

_____

_____

_____

_____

_____

What's going on when those struggles come up? (Where are you? What are you thinking about? Who's around?)

_____

_____

_____

_____

What does the above Scripture say about this struggle? Who can help you with it?

_____

_____

_____

_____

_____

# ANALYSIS

Why do you think these sins still get to you?

_____

_____

_____

# W1-D1 READ LUKE 22:60-62.

Now, put yourself in Peter's shoes. How would you react after the rooster crowed? Why?

_____

_____

_____

_____

What kind of expression would be on Jesus' face if you could see Him physically at any given point in your day—watching you make certain choices right in front of Him?

_____

_____

_____

_____

# ACTION

Name at least two things you can do to protect yourself from getting into situations that lead you to give in to sin.

_____

_____

_____

_____

**READ JAMES 1:6-8.** How will you rely on God to help you? Do you really believe He will help you leave these sins behind? If not, how could you resolve your doubt?

_____

_____

_____

_____

**TODAY, IF YOU HEAR HIS VOICE,** do not harden your hearts . . . See to it, brothers, that none of you has a sinful, unbelieving heart that turns away from the living God. But encourage one another daily, as long as it is called Today, so that none of you may be hardened by sin's deceitfulness.

—**Hebrews 3:7–8, 12–13**

**IN YOUR RISE UP: TRAINING MANUAL,** you wrote down the different kinds of media and cultural elements that had numbed your senses to godly conviction. Take a moment to think again about what influences you.

# INSPECTION

What were your standards for media content before going through basic training? What habits did you change as a result of the *Rise Up* experience?

_____

_____

_____

_____

According to the above Scripture, what causes people to turn away from God?

_____

_____

_____

_____

# W1-D2 ANALYSIS

**HOW DO MEDIA** choices affect a person's outlook and attitudes? How have they affected you? Your relationship with God?

_____

_____

_____

**IF YOU KNOW YOU'VE MADE** choices that have damaged your faith and moral standards, but haven't changed anything about the types of media you take in, why not? What does God have to say about that?
(See James 1:22–25.)

_____

_____

_____

# ACTION

What do you need to do to stay committed to God's principles for purity—and to be aware when you edge toward compromise?

_____

_____

_____

How will you keep your heart soft toward God? (Feel free to describe your feelings in doodles, not just words. Use the notes pages at the end of the chapter if you need to.)

_____

_____

_____

_____

# MENTAL MANAGEMENT

**THEREFORE, I URGE YOU, BROTHERS,** in view of God's mercy, to offer your bodies as living sacrifices, holy and pleasing to God—this is your spiritual act of worship. Do not conform any longer to the pattern of this world, but be transformed by the renewing of your mind. Then you will be able to test and approve what God's will is—his good, pleasing, and perfect will.

—Romans 12:1-2

**YOUR RISE UP: TRAINING MANUAL** included a page that gave you a real gut check. It listed questions asking about attitudes and actions that are considered to be sin. To refresh your memory, here's that list one more time:

- ☐ Do I despise anyone?
- ☐ Am I a jealous person?
- ☐ Do I lie?
- ☐ Do I put anything or anyone before God?
- ☐ Do I ever swear?
- ☐ Do I honor my parents?
- ☐ Do I honor God with my body?
- ☐ Am I greedy?
- ☐ Am I a complainer?
- ☐ Am I bitter?
- ☐ Do I tell dirty jokes?
- ☐ Do I get drunk?
- ☐ Do I indulge in impure thoughts?
- ☐ What else?

What items on this list reflect choices you are currently making?

_____

_____

_____

_____

**READ PROVERBS 15:26.** How does God feel about the choices we make in our thought life? What does this tell you about God? (See Philippians 4:8.)

_____

_____

_____

_____

**READ HEBREWS 10:16.** What does God promise to do for us in this area? What is our responsibility in this?

_____

_____

_____

_____

_____

# ANALYSIS

**READ MATTHEW 12:25.** How does this verse apply to your relationship with God as it pertains to your thought life?

_____

_____

_____

_____

When asked which is the greatest commandment, Jesus replied, "Love the Lord your God with all your heart and with all your soul and with all your mind" (Matt. 22:37). Why do you think He said this? What does it mean to you to do this? How could it change your life?

_____

_____

_____

_____

# ACTION

The Bible tells us to "fix [our] thoughts on Jesus" (Heb. 3:1). How will you begin to do this today?

_____

_____

_____

_____

_____

Where do you need to build thought boundaries? Suggest two ways your *Rise Up* partner and accountability advisor can help you with this.

_____

_____

_____

_____

_____

# LETTERS TO GOD

**EVERYONE WHO SINS BREAKS THE LAW;** in fact, sin is lawlessness. But you know that he appeared so that he might take away our sins. And in him is no sin. No one who lives in him keeps on sinning. No one who continues to sin has either seen him or known him.

—1 John 3:4–6

**HAVE MERCY** on me, O God,
according to your unfailing love;
according to your great compassion
blot out my transgressions.
Wash away all my iniquity
and cleanse me from my sin.

For I know my transgressions,
and my sin is always before me.

—Psalm 51:1–3

**REMEMBER THE LETTER** you wrote to God during your *Rise Up* experience? You were laying it all on the line, asking Him to help you give up sins that had taken hold in your heart. (If you weren't ready at that time to write this letter, you may want to use today's study time and write it now). We're going to take some time to look at the power of a repentant heart.

# INSPECTION

The word "repent" literally means "to turn around." What does God want us to do when He calls us to repent? (Hint: see Joel 2:12–13.)

_____

_____

_____

_____

**LUKE 15:11–24** tells the story of a young man who had to learn about repentance the hard way. How does God respond when we choose to leave sinful habits and lifestyles? What does this mean to you?

_____

_____

_____

_____

According to 1 Corinthians 10:13, how does God help us when temptation strikes?

_____

_____

_____

_____

Think of a time when God provided a "way out" of temptation for you. Write or doodle about this experience. (Flip to the open pages at the end of the week if you need more space to express yourself.)

_____

_____

_____

# ANALYSIS

God has given us a spirit of power, of love, and of self-discipline (2 Tim. 1:7). Why is it important to know this truth?

_____

_____

_____

_____

_____

Jesus never sinned, but He was tempted in every way we are—and suffered. As you come to the Lord for help in giving up sin, how does this fact impact the way you think about or relate to Him?

_____

_____

_____

_____

_____

# ACTION

**READ 1 SAMUEL 7:3.** What will total commitment to God look like in your life? What idols will you need to repent of for this to happen?

_____

_____

_____

_____

_____

# UNFINISHED BUSINESS

**I TELL YOU THAT** . . . there will be more rejoicing in heaven over one sinner who repents than over ninety-nine righteous persons who do not need to repent.

**—Luke 15:7**

**AFTER YOU WROTE** your letter to God, you had a few minutes to write down the specific things you repented of, as well as the things you planned to change in your life to reflect that. You also had a chance to write down sins you didn't feel ready to surrender to Him—and why.

# INSPECTION

A rich young ruler turned away from Jesus because there were things in his life that he wasn't willing to give up (Matt. 19:21–22). What elements in your life are keeping you from following Jesus 100 percent?

_____

_____

_____

_____

_____

John the Baptist urged the religious leaders of his time to "produce fruit in keeping with repentance" (Matt. 3:8). What does this kind of fruit look like? (See Galatians 5:22–24.)

_____

_____

_____

**W1-D5**    **ACTS 26:20** describes the proof that a person has truly repented: "they should repent and turn to God and prove their repentance by their deeds." You expressed repentance of certain sins during basic training. What evidence of true repentance have you shown since then?

_____

_____

_____

_____

_____

_____

_____

# ANALYSIS

According to the apostle Paul, godly sorrow brings repentance, but worldly sorrow brings death (2 Cor. 7:10). What is the difference between godly sorrow and worldly sorrow?

_____

_____

_____

_____

_____

_____

What kind of "sorrow" is evident in your life? What does this say about your relationship with God?

_____

_____

_____

_____

_____

# ACTION

Jesus died to set us free from the slavery of sin. We must choose to stand firm and not let ourselves be slaves to sin any longer (Gal. 5:1). Write at least two things you can do to stand firm in your commitment to resist temptation and give up the sins that have been present in your life.

_____

_____

_____

_____

_____

_____

_____

_____

**PSALM 119:11** and **GALATIANS 5:16** give us two key actions that help us live out our repentance. What are they? What steps will you take to start living your life this way?

_____

_____

_____

_____

_____

_____

_____

_____

NOTES

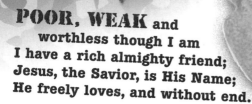

POOR, WEAK and worthless though I am
I have a rich almighty friend;
Jesus, the Savior, is His Name;
He freely loves, and without end.

He ransomed me from hell with blood,
And by His power my foes controlled;
He found me wandering far from God,
And brought me to His chosen fold.
—John Newton

**THE SECOND SESSION OF RISE UP: BASIC TRAINING FOR WARRIORS** introduced you to (drum roll please) . . . yourself. You learned where feelings of self-doubt and worthlessness come from and how they affect the choices you make.

You also learned that you can't follow Christ's commandment to love others as yourself until you love yourself—and that you can only come to this place when you understand and receive the **LORD'S EXTRAVAGANT LOVE FOR YOU.**

Both God and Satan know what you're really worth: the price of Jesus' precious blood, spilled for your sake and your sins. **GOD HAS PROVIDED ALL YOU NEED** to discover your identity in Christ. Satan will throw at you every lie he can think of to keep you from getting to that point.

What are you believing today? **HAVE YOU BEEN SOAKING UP GOD'S TRUTH —OR SATAN'S LIES?**

## THIS WEEK'S MEMORY VERSE

**MEMORIZE . . .**

How great is the love the Father has lavished on us, that we should be called children of God!

—1 John 3:1

**REMIND YOURSELF** every day this week that you are a child of the Father.

**TURN BACK** to this page throughout the week.

What comes to your mind as you say this verse? Draw it as a picture below.

**FOR HE CHOSE US IN HIM** before the creation of the world to be holy and blameless in his sight. In love he predestined us to be adopted as his sons through Jesus Christ, in accordance with his pleasure and will—to the praise of his glorious grace, which he has freely given us in the One he loves. In him we have redemption through his blood, the forgiveness of sins, in accordance with the riches of God's grace that he lavished on us with all wisdom and understanding.

—Ephesians 1:4–8

## DURING THIS SESSION OF BASIC TRAINING,

you wrote in your training manual the lies you've been believing about yourself. Then you jotted down where you learned these lies and how they influence you. Sometimes they can influence you enough to cause you to harm yourself. God wants to free you from the chains of these thought patterns!

# INSPECTION

Are there some lies that still have a hold on you? Think for a minute. They usually surface when you make a mistake, when someone says something unkind to you, or you compare yourself to someone else (even an airbrushed magazine photo). Describe those lies here.

_____

_____

_____

_____

_____

**READ EPHESIANS 3:16-19.** What does this passage say about the love of Christ? What do we need in order to comprehend this love?

_____

_____

_____

_____

_____

_____

# ANALYSIS

God promises that He will never reject us (Ps. 94:14). How is this thought significant to you?

_____

_____

_____

_____

_____

_____

_____

As Christians, we are "a chosen people, a royal priesthood, a holy nation, a people belonging to God" (1 Peter 2:9). Compare this to the things you currently believe about yourself.

_____

_____

_____

_____

_____

_____

# W2-D1

Think about your relationship with God. How do the things you believe about yourself—positive or negative—show up in your interactions with Him?

_____

_____

_____

_____

_____

# ACTION

If there are still barriers between you and the Lord today, what can you do to break them down?

_____

_____

_____

_____

_____

In the same way, in what ways could you strengthen the areas in which you feel confident and open with God?

_____

_____

_____

_____

_____

**THE LORD YOUR GOD** is with you,
he is mighty to save.
He will take great delight in you,
he will quiet you with his love,
he will rejoice over you with singing.

—Zephaniah 3:17

**GOD HAS A LOT TO SAY** about your value, and you learned some of it during the Rise Up experience. We're going to list them again below:

■ **WHEN YOU WANT TO RUN AWAY** and hide from everything in life, God is the only one to run to who can protect you (Deut. 33:27).

■ You are the **APPLE OF GOD'S EYE** (Ps. 17:8).

■ He is good and His love for you **ENDURES FOREVER** (Ps. 100:5).

■ His banner over you is **LOVE** (Song of Songs 2:4).

■ His **UNFAILING LOVE** for you will never be shaken—He has compassion for you (Is.54:10).

■ **HIS LOVE FOR YOU** is endless and His mercies are new every day (Lam. 3:22–23).

■ **HE DIED FOR YOU** while you were still a sinner [while you were still turning your back on Him] (Rom. 5:8).

■ We can't fully comprehend all that **GOD HAS PREPARED** for those who love Him (1 Cor. 2:9).

■ **GOD LAVISHES HIS LOVE** on you, calling you His child (1 John 3:1).

■ Even if your heart condemns you, **GOD IS GREATER** than your heart and does not condemn you (1 John 3:19–20).

# W2-D2 INSPECTION

In your *Rise Up: Training Manual*, you wrote down three words that describe how you see yourself. What would you write today?

_____

_____

_____

_____

_____

_____

What does **LUKE 12:6-7** say about sparrows—and about you?

_____

_____

_____

_____

_____

# ANALYSIS

**READ ISAIAH 40:11.** Describe what this verse communicates to you about God's feelings for you.

_____

_____

_____

_____

Look at the three words you wrote about yourself in the "Inspection" area. Why did you choose these words?

_____

_____

_____

_____

# ACTION

What is God saying to you today? How do you plan to respond to Him?

_____

_____

_____

_____

_____

_____

_____

_____

Finish today's study by reading **JEREMIAH 31:3-4.**

_____

_____

_____

_____

_____

_____

_____

_____

**BUT NOW, THIS IS WHAT THE LORD SAYS—** he who created you, O Jacob, he who formed you, O Israel: "Fear not, for I have redeemed you; I have summoned you by name; you are mine. When you pass through the waters, I will be with you; and when pass through the rivers, they will not sweep over you. When you walk through the fire, you will not be burned; the flames will not set you ablaze. For I am the Lord, your God, the Holy One of Israel, your Savior; I give Egypt for your ransom, Cush and Seba in your stead. Since you are precious and honored in my sight, and because I love you, I will give men in exchange for you, and people in exchange for your life. Do not be afraid, for I am with you; I will bring your children from the east and gather you from the west. . . . You are my witnesses," declares the Lord, "and my servant whom I have chosen, so that you may know and believe me and understand that I am he. Before me no god was formed, nor will there be one after me."

**—Isaiah 43:1–5, 10**

Today we'll be looking again at what God says about you. During **BASIC TRAINING FOR WARRIORS,** you learned six key statements from the Bible:

**1.** You were created in His image (Gen. 1:27).
**2.** You are one of His children (1 John 3:1).
**3.** You are His choice possession (James 1:18, NLT).
**4.** You can do all things through Christ (Phil. 4:13).
**5.** You are full of wisdom (1 Cor. 1:30).
**6.** You are fearfully and wonderfully made (Ps. 139:14).

When Jesus chose someone to be His disciple, He called to them and said "Follow me." How did Jesus invite you to follow Him?

_____

_____

_____

_____

_____

_____

_____

**READ JEREMIAH 29:11.** What are God's intentions toward you?

_____

_____

_____

_____

_____

# ANALYSIS

**READ 2 THESSALONIANS 2:13.** What does it mean to be chosen?

_____

_____

_____

_____

_____

_____

_____

**W2-D3** To what degree do you truly believe that God has chosen you to be His child? If you feel some doubt, write down what it is you are unsure of. Then spend some time reading Isaiah 43:10.

_____

_____

_____

_____

_____

_____

# ACTION

**EPHESIANS 5:1** and **JOHN 15:16** describe two expectations God has of His chosen people. What are they? Give several examples of how you can put these commands into practice.

_____

_____

_____

_____

_____

Choose one of your examples and do it this week. (Make it stand out from the others above by putting a star next to it.) Ask your basic training partner and accountability advisor to check in with you on your follow-through.

_____

_____

_____

_____

_____

**BUT WHEN HE,** the Spirit of truth comes, he will guide you into all truth. **John 16:13a**

**REMEMBER HOW YOU** "undid the lies" in Session Two of *Rise Up?* You wrote out the lies you had been believing about your identity and worth—and, with the help of a friend, turned the tables on them. One of the members of your youth group took your manual and rewrote each lie, turning it into a reflection of God's truth.

# INSPECTION

We've already established that Satan doesn't want you to know who you are in Christ. What does Jesus have to say about him in John 8:44?

_____

_____

_____

_____

_____

What does I John 4:1 tell us to do?

_____

_____

_____

_____

_____

_____

_____

# W2-D4 ANALYSIS

Have you ever been to a carnival fun house? They often feature a room filled with warped and oddly shaped mirrors. Those mirrors show distorted reflections. To see ourselves as we really are, we need to look into a perfectly flat mirror.

_____

_____

_____

As the father of lies, Satan distorts our perspective of ourselves. But Christ, being perfect, shows us the truth. What kind of reflection are you seeing right now?

_____

_____

_____

**READ MATTHEW 6:22–23.** Why do you think the lies you struggled with have had such a strong grip on you?

_____

_____

_____

_____

# ACTION

Look at your notes from the "Inspection" section of this week's first day of study. Copy down the lies you said you still believe. Then, using the review verses from yesterday's study, write down the truths that cancel out those lies.

_____

_____

# TUG OF WAR
## MAKE IT REAL

**WHATEVER YOU HAVE LEARNED** or received or heard from me, or seen in me—put it into practice. And the God of peace will be with you.

**Philippians 4:9**

**WHEN YOU WERE** finishing the "Who Are You" session during *Rise Up,* your youth group leader gave you some time to let the truths you had learned about God and about yourself sink in. By doing this, you let God engrave your I.D. tag and refused to let the world scribble its lies next to your name any longer. We're going to give you time to revisit these truths again today.

## INSPECTION

From Day Two of this week's study, write down three things God says about your value that strike a chord inside your heart.

_____
_____
_____
_____
_____
_____
_____
_____

**W2-D5** Now, from Day Three, write down two things God says about who you are that mean the most to you.

_____

_____

_____

_____

_____

_____

_____

# ANALYSIS

Take the five statements you chose and plug each one into this sentence:

Because God says _____, I am/can _____.

Write out those five sentences here:

_____

_____

_____

_____

_____

_____

_____

_____

_____

_____

_____

_____

_____

_____

_____

How did you get to know God better this week?
What are you seeing differently about yourself?

_____

_____

_____

_____

_____

_____

_____

# ACTION

Write down your favorite Scripture verses from this week's
study onto index cards and memorize them. Tape your cards up
in your bedroom or your bathroom, carry them in your school-
books, or stick them on the inside door of your locker.

_____

_____

_____

_____

_____

_____

_____

_____

_____

_____

_____

_____

_____

_____

_____

_____

**EVIL NEVER SURRENDERS** its grasp without a tremendous fight. We never arrive at any spiritual inheritance through the enjoyment of a picnic, but always through the fierce conflicts of the battlefield.

—John Henry Jowett

**ADDICTIONS.** They're the things you can't say "no" to. The things that seem to have control over your thoughts and choices. The things that keep you catering to them **INSTEAD OF SERVING GOD.**

**YOUR YOUTH GROUP HIT THIS TOPIC PRETTY HARD** during *Rise Up.* You learned that addictions come in many forms, from drug use to shopping to sex. And you learned that you needed to identify these toxins in your own life so they could be flushed out of your system—**SPIRITUALLY, MENTALLY, EMOTIONALLY, AND PHYSICALLY.**

Maybe you accepted the challenge of beginning a detox for yourself. Maybe you didn't. Either way, this week you'll be making choices once again—**TO SAY YES TO GOD . . . OR TO YOURSELF.**

**MEMORIZE . . .**

I have hidden your word in my heart
that I might not sin against you.

—Psalm 119:11

**HIDE GOD'S WORD** in your heart this week.

**USE THIS SPACE** to write out Psalm 119:11. Spend time every day this week committing it to memory.

**LIKE A CITY WHOSE** walls are broken down is a man who lacks self-control.

—**Proverbs 25:28**

**IN YOUR TRAINING MANUAL** you began to identify your personal addictions. This was your first step toward freedom: identifying the enemy. That thing may have begun as something innocent, but now it's dominating you. And now it's time to put God back where He belongs—on the throne of your heart.

# INSPECTION

What were your definitions of "addiction" and "idol" before you went through the *Rise Up* weekend? Give some examples:

_____

_____

_____

_____

_____

# ANALYSIS

During basic training, you listed the things you couldn't say "no" to, what habits came to mind that you had never considered to be "idols" before?

_____

_____

_____

**READ PROVERBS 28:13-14** and **1 PETER 4:7.** Why is it important to identify and renounce, or cast off, addictive sins?

_____

_____

_____

_____

How has your perspective and awareness of this issue changed in the weeks since basic training? At school? At home?

_____

_____

_____

_____

_____

# ACTION

## READ 1 THESSALONIANS 5:5-8. What have you been doing to practice self-control in areas of your life where you are tempted?

_____

_____

_____

_____

_____

Write down two questions you want your accountability partner to ask you regularly regarding the addictions you're kicking.

_____

_____

_____

**IN MY DISTRESS** I called to the LORD;
I cried to my God for help.
From his temple he heard my voice;
my cry came before him, into his ears . . . .
He reached down from on high
and took hold of me;
he drew me out of deep waters.
He rescued me from my powerful enemy,
from my foes, who were too strong for me.
—Psalm 18:6, 16–17

**IN THE NEXT SEGMENT** of "The Things You Couldn't Say No To," you identified the temptation that's the toughest for you to resist. Then you chose an even tougher truth from the Bible that you could use to combat that enticing idea. You were learning, in a very practical way, how to stand on God's Word.

# INSPECTION

What temptation did you identify as your deadliest spiritual enemy?

_____

_____

_____

_____

_____

_____

_____

_____

What Scripture did you feel would help you resist that enemy? (If you don't remember, this is your cue to find another one.)

_____

_____

_____

_____

# ANALYSIS

Read the verses from Psalm 18 again. As you learned during basic training, one of the ways we can call to the Lord for help is by applying the Bible to our situation. In Ephesians 6:17, the Word of God is referred to as "the sword of the Spirit." How have you put your sword to use since basic training? How have you seen God helping you through your chosen Scripture?

_____

_____

_____

_____

_____

In this week's memory verse, the Psalmist wrote: "I have hidden your word in my heart that I might not sin against you" (Ps. 119:11). What does it mean to hide God's Word in your heart? How is this different from simply quoting Bible verses?

_____

_____

_____

_____

**W3-D2** Describe the condition of a Christian heart that has been nourished with God's Word. Contrast these thoughts with a Christian heart that has not been filled with Scripture. (Feel free to use your notes pages to draw a picture of your ideas).

_____

_____

_____

_____

_____

_____

_____

_____

# ACTION

**REVIEW PROVERBS 28:13.** If you still haven't acknowledged the addictive sins in your life, now is a good time to do so. Whether for follow-up or for first-time sharing, talk with your accountability advisor about how you did with today's study. They will help you take steps toward the freedom only God can give to you!

_____

_____

_____

_____

_____

_____

_____

_____

_____

# MAKE YOUR CHOICE

**...CHOOSE FOR YOURSELVES** this day whom you will serve... But as for me and my household, we will serve the LORD.                    Joshua 24:15

**THE NEXT CONCEPT** you focused on as you confronted your addictions was *choice*. In your student guide, you studied five key choices you will need to make to overcome these issues:

**PRAY**
**CHOOSE** your friends wisely
**TALK** to a close friend every time you are tempted
**KNOW** what the Bible says
**CHANGE** the way you do things

**THESE CHOICES ARE NOT MAGIC FORMULAS,** but tools and strategies you can use to learn how to consistently gain victory over the addictive sins in your life.

# INSPECTION

Which of the above strategies have you implemented since the *Rise Up* experience?

_____

_____

_____

_____

_____

_____

_____

# W3-D3 ANALYSIS

Of the five steps listed above, which has been the easiest to practice? Which has been the hardest?

_____

_____

_____

_____

_____

_____

**PROVERBS 22:3** says, "A prudent man sees danger and takes refuge, but the simple keep going and suffer for it." Since experiencing basic training, in what ways have you chosen to take refuge from temptation? In what ways have you chosen to put yourself in vulnerable positions? How did both of these choices impact your relationship with God?

_____

_____

_____

_____

_____

_____

Describe how **PSALM 73:2, 25-26** apply to you.

_____

_____

_____

_____

_____

_____

_____

# ACTION

**PROVERBS 4:27** reminds us to keep ourselves from doing evil. What has been your most successful strategy in accomplishing this?

_____

_____

_____

_____

_____

_____

_____

_____

_____

_____

**NOW READ PROVERBS 27:17.** If you have found success in overcoming addictive sins, how could you help a friend sharpen their edge in their own battle against temptation?

_____

_____

_____

_____

_____

_____

_____

_____

_____

_____

_____

# WEEK THREE DAY FOUR: CUTTING OFF THE ENEMY

**IF YOUR RIGHT EYE CAUSES YOU TO SIN,** gouge it out and throw it away. It is better for you to lose one part of your body than for your whole body to be thrown into hell.
—**Matthew 5:29**

**DURING BASIC TRAINING,** you cut off the enemy altogether by agreeing to a month-long media fast. This was one major boundary—resisting some of the elements that cause you to stumble by shutting them out of your life for a whole month.

When a wound develops gangrene, the injured person can die from those toxins. **TO SAVE A LIFE,** doctors sometimes have to sacrifice a limb. This media fast was a type of amputation. That's what the above verse from Matthew means, and that's what you did by cutting yourself off from media. You took a major source of spiritual and emotional poison in your life and eliminated it, keeping it from wounding you any deeper.

# INSPECTION

What was your initial reaction to the "media fast challenge"?

_____

_____

_____

_____

_____

_____

If you chose to accept the challenge, describe your experience here. (Remember, you can describe it in doodles, not just words! Use the extra space provided on your notes pages if you need to.)

_____

_____

_____

_____

_____

# ANALYSIS

What was/is the hardest part about this fast? In other words, what form of media did you miss the most?

_____

_____

_____

_____

Did you "cheat" at all during the fast? If so, in what area and why? Ephesians 4:27 says: "Do not give the devil a foothold." How did he get a foothold in this area of your life?

_____

_____

_____

If you chose not to participate in the media fast, why not? Do you think you could make the commitment now, even in one area?

_____

_____

_____

_____

# W3-D4 ACTION

In Bible times, a city's primary defense was the tall, thick walls that surrounded it. If the walls fell, the city fell. (See Joshua 6:20.) How will you continue to cut off the enemy's access to your heart? What kind of walls do you need to keep building so your enemy doesn't get a foothold into your life again?

_____

_____

_____

_____

_____

_____

_____

_____

_____

_____

_____

_____

_____

_____

_____

_____

**IF I HAD CHERISHED SIN IN MY HEART,**
the LORD would not have listened;
but God has surely listened
and heard my voice in prayer.
Praise be to God,
who has not rejected my prayer
or withheld his love from me!

—Psalm 66:18-20

**DURING BASIC TRAINING,** the last step you took on the journey to freedom was to anchor yourself to God's Word. You took the Scripture you chose to battle addictive sin with and wrote it down again. You thought about it, what it meant, and how you were going to stand on its truth when you went home.

**TODAY'S STUDY IS A BIT DIFFERENT.** You're going to be writing down some more Scriptures that will help you to gain victory against temptation. Look up each Scripture and write it out. As you write it, say it out loud so your mind doesn't wander. **REALLY TUNE IN TO THESE TRUTHS.** Choose to stand firm in your faith!

# 2 CHRONICLES 20:12, 17 AND 22

_____
_____
_____
_____
_____
_____
_____

## PSALM 20:7-8

_____
_____
_____
_____
_____
_____
_____

## PSALM 40:2-3

_____
_____
_____
_____
_____

## PSALM 37:23-24

_____
_____
_____
_____
_____

## 1 CORINTHIANS 15:58

_____
_____
_____
_____
_____

## 1 CORINTHIANS 16:13

_____
_____
_____
_____
_____

# I PETER 5:8-9

_____
_____
_____
_____
_____
_____

# GALATIANS 5:1

_____
_____
_____
_____
_____
_____
_____

# ISAIAH 7:9

_____
_____
_____
_____
_____
_____
_____

# MATTHEW 12:25

_____
_____
_____
_____
_____
_____
_____

_____

_____

_____

_____

_____

_____

_____

# ACTION

Choose the Scripture above that is the most helpful as you fight to beat temptation. What can you do during the next week to cement this truth into your heart? What in your life will be different when you live according to this Scripture?

_____

_____

_____

_____

_____

_____

_____

_____

_____

_____

_____

_____

_____

_____

_____

NOTES

**A REAL FRIEND** is one who helps us to think our best thoughts, do our noblest deeds, and be our finest selves.

—Unknown

**FORGIVENESS IS THE FRAGRANCE** the violet sheds on the heel that has crushed it.

—Mark Twain

**SESSION FOUR OF BASIC TRAINING** put your relationships with friends under the microscope. You took a long, hard look at what kind of influence your friends have over you – positive or negative. You thought about whether you were harboring feelings of unforgiveness toward any of them, and whether you needed to go ask someone to forgive you for hurting them.

This session also pushed you to **BE HONEST WITH YOURSELF** about the quality of your relationships with family members. You needed to consider the **"FORGIVENESS FACTOR"** with them, too. To get some perspective, you were reminded of what Jesus did for you on the cross and how freely He forgave you. Then you had a chance to express your forgiveness by releasing a helium balloon. **EASY ENOUGH, RIGHT?**

**WRONG**. Some time has passed since you evaluated these friendships and sent that balloon into the sky. The pull of peer pressure and the sting of misunderstandings at home can make our best intentions falter. Where is your resolve today? How's your heart today? **DO THESE DECISIONS NEED SOME REVIVING?**

### MEMORIZE . . .

And let us consider how we may spur one another on toward love and good deeds.

—Hebrews 10:24

**PUT HEBREWS 10:24** into action in all of your friendships this week.

**CHALLENGE YOURSELF** to memorize this verse by saying it into the mirror five times a day. (Have fun!)

# WEEK FOUR DAY ONE: FRIEND OR STUMBLING BLOCK?

**IF . . . YOUR CLOSEST FRIEND SECRETLY** entices you, saying, "Let us go and worship other gods" (gods that neither you nor you fathers have known, gods of the peoples around you, whether near or far, from one end of the land to the other), do not yield to him or listen to him.
—Deuteronomy 13:6–8

**YOUR FIRST ASSIGNMENT** in Session Four of *Rise Up: Basic Training for Warriors* was to list the names of your friends in order of their closeness to you. The challenge of this assignment was to either acknowledge how your friends encourage you to grow close to God—or admit how they pull you away from Him.

If you keep reading the above passage in Deuteronomy, you might be shocked by what it says next: "Stone him to death, because he tried to turn you away from the Lord your God" (v. 10).

**NOW, DON'T FREAK OUT!** Today we live under the grace of Jesus Christ and not under the law of Moses. What God wants you to know as a Christian teen living in the 21st century is that He takes your relationship with Him seriously. And He expects you to do the same—in part, by choosing friends who won't lead you into sin.

# INSPECTION

Think about that list of friends you named. You took some notes on which friendships would be worth building up and which friendships might need to fade away. Where are those friendships at today?

_____

_____

_____

_____

_____

_____

_____

_____

_____

Which of your friendships reflect this week's memory verse: Hebrews 10:24?

_____

_____

_____

_____

_____

_____

In contrast, which friendships look more like 1 Corinthians 15:33?

_____

_____

_____

_____

_____

# ANALYSIS

**PROVERBS 27:6 SAYS:** "Wounds from a friend can be trusted, but an enemy multiplies kisses." (Some translations say that an enemy's kisses are full of lies.) Write this verse in your own words. How do you see it happening in your current friendships?

_____

_____

_____

_____

_____

**READ 1 THESSALONIANS 5:11.** In what areas do you need godly friends to do this for you? How could you do this for them?

_____

_____

_____

_____

_____

_____

# ACTION

What steps will you take to develop friendships with the strong Christians in your life?

_____

_____

_____

_____

_____

**. . . LET YOUR LIGHT SHINE** before men, that they may see your good deeds and praise your Father in heaven.
—Matthew 5:16

**THEREFORE, IF YOU ARE OFFERING YOUR GIFT** at the altar and there remember that your brother has something against you, leave your gift there in front of the altar. First go and be reconciled with your brother; then come and offer your gift.
—Matthew 5:23–24

**YOUR NEXT TASK** in Session Four of *Rise Up: Basic Training for Warriors* was to look at the example you've been setting in your friendships. You had to think about the quality of your influence (or lack thereof) on non-Christians, as well as the quality of your interactions with fellow believers.

**THIS ASSIGNMENT WAS A LESSON** in humility. It can be hard to admit our flaws and failures, can't it? Today's study is designed to help you continue to raise your standards closer to Christ-like behavior.

# INSPECTION

In your training manual you wrote down the name of at least one friend you haven't shared your faith with yet, and why. Have you talked to that person about Jesus? If you have, what did you say? How did he or she respond?

**W4-D2** If you haven't done this yet, write down what you would like this person to know about the Lord and about your relationship with Him.

_____

_____

_____

_____

_____

_____

_____

You also were encouraged to take care of any conflicts you were experiencing with members of your youth group. Describe what you did to set things right, whether you needed to receive or extend forgiveness.

_____

_____

_____

_____

_____

_____

_____

# ANALYSIS

**READ MATTHEW 5:23-24 AGAIN.** Why does Jesus give this instruction? What does this tell you about God?

_____

_____

_____

_____

_____

Peter and John, two of Jesus' disciples, are shown boldly sharing their faith in Acts 4:8–13. Take a look at this passage and write down three points that you feel could help you share your testimony.

_____

_____

_____

_____

_____

_____

# ACTION

**1 TIMOTHY 4:12 SAYS:** "Don't let anyone look down on you because you are young, but set an example for the believers in speech, in life, in love, in faith, and in purity." Name one way you could set a godly example in each of the areas listed in this verse.

_____

_____

_____

_____

_____

_____

_____

This month, look for an opportunity to share with your non-Christian friend the thoughts you wrote about Jesus in Inspection Question #2.

_____

_____

_____

_____

_____

# FRIENDS WHO HELP YOU UP

**IF ONE FALLS DOWN,** his friend can help him up.
**But pity the man who falls and has no one to help him up!**
—Ecclesiastes 4:10

**IT'S EASY TO KEEP YOUR RELATIONSHIPS** in a "safe," shallow place when you only see people at church and youth group. But as Christians, we need the fellowship and support of other believers to help us navigate the sometimes-stormy waters of our journey with God. That's why your youth group leader booted you out of your comfort zone during this session of your basic training experience.

At this stage in the weekend, you chose your *Extreme Commitment* partner and your accountability advisor—a Christian peer and a Christian adult you felt you could trust with these tough-to-talk-about issues and prayer requests.

# INSPECTION

What was your initial reaction to the requirement to seek believers to keep you accountable?

_____

_____

_____

_____

_____

_____

_____

What do Hebrews 5:14 and I Timothy 4:7–8 say about spiritual training?

W4-D3

_____
_____
_____
_____
_____
_____

# ANALYSIS

**PROVERBS 19:20 SAYS:** "Listen to advice and accept instruction, and in the end you will be wise." What's the most helpful piece of advice you've received so far from your accountability advisor? On the flip side, what's been the most difficult feedback to swallow?

_____
_____
_____
_____
_____
_____

What qualities in your accountability advisor would you like to develop in yourself?

_____
_____
_____
_____
_____
_____

OVER THE EDGE

9

**W4-D3** How is your accountability partner helping you develop the character traits described in Galatians 5:22–23?

_____

_____

_____

_____

_____

_____

_____

_____

_____

_____

# ACTION

Name one way you can continue to deepen your relationship with each of your accountability helpers.

_____

_____

_____

_____

_____

_____

_____

**THEREFORE, AS GOD'S CHOSEN** people, holy and dearly loved, clothe yourselves with compassion, kindness, humility, gentleness, and patience. Bear with each other and forgive whatever grievances you may have against one another. Forgive as the Lord forgave you. And over all these virtues put on love, which binds them all together in perfect unity.

—Colossians 3:12–14

**AFTER YOU SPENT TIME EVALUATING** and renewing friendships and learning about spiritual accountability, your youth group leader turned your attention to family. You may recall being reminded that no matter how positive our home environments may be, people are still human. They have a tendency to disappoint and hurt each other, and family members in particular can sometimes cause our deepest wounds.

This part of Session Four delved deeper into the **MEANING AND IMPORTANCE OF FORGIVENESS.** It was a time to understand that holding a grudge leaves the conflict unresolved and your spirit embittered. It was a time to acknowledge what family members you needed to forgive. And it was a time to receive God's unfailing love.

# INSPECTION

In your training manual, you noted the names of family members you needed to have a heart-to-heart talk with about the hurt they have caused you. Did you have those talks? What did you say? How did they respond?

_____

_____

_____

**W4-D4** You also noted family members you know you had offended, writing down what you intended to change about your behavior toward them. Describe how this decision has changed your relationship with those relatives.

_____
_____
_____
_____
_____
_____

# ANALYSIS

When Jesus told His disciples to forgive their brother seven times in a day if he expressed repentance for offending them, they said: "Increase our faith!" (Luke 17:3–5). Why is it so difficult for people to forgive each other?

_____
_____
_____
_____
_____
_____
_____

If you're holding a grudge against a family member, how could that bitterness affect your relationship with God?

_____
_____
_____
_____
_____

**READ THE STORY** of the unforgiving servant (Matt. 18:23–35). What perspective does this give you on forgiveness?

_____

_____

_____

_____

_____

_____

# ACTION

How will you demonstrate the principles of Ephesians 4:31–32 to your family this week?

_____

_____

_____

_____

_____

_____

_____

# RELEASE

**WHEN JOSEPH'S BROTHERS SAW** that their father was dead, they said: "What if Joseph holds a grudge against us and pays us back for all the wrongs we did to him?" So they sent word to Joseph, saying, "Your father left these instructions before he died: 'This is what you are to say to Joseph: I ask you to forgive your brothers the sins and the wrongs they committed in treating you so badly.' Now please forgive the sins of the servants of the God of your father." When their message came to him, Joseph wept. His brothers then came and threw themselves down before him. "We are your slaves," they said. But Joseph said to them, "Don't be afraid. Am I in the place of God? You intended to harm me, but God intended it for good to accomplish what is now being done, the saving of many lives. So then, don't be afraid. I will provide for you and your children." And he reassured them and spoke kindly to them.

—Genesis 50:15-21

**THIS FINAL SEGMENT** of Session Four gave you the opportunity to put some of these forgiveness lessons into practice. You had a chance to go to the front of your youth group's meeting room to express forgiveness for hurts caused by friends and family. If your need was to repent of things you had done to hurt these people, you could express that, too. Then, symbolically, you took communion to remember the terrible price Jesus paid for your own sins.

Afterward, you wrote down the names of people whom you forgave, attached them to a balloon, and released it into the sky.

These types of symbolic actions can help cement the miracles that are happening in our spirits when God touches us deeply. However, you have still had some choices to make since that time.

# INSPECTION

What emotions did you feel as you took communion and released your "forgiveness balloon"?

_____

_____

_____

_____

Describe the power of forgiveness as seen in the life of Esau (Gen. 27:41 and Gen. 33:4).

_____

_____

_____

_____

# ANALYSIS

What's the difference between feeling like you have forgiven someone and knowing that you have?

_____

_____

_____

_____

How do you practice forgiveness? Consider the words of Corrie ten Boom: "Forgiveness is an act of the will, and the will can function regardless of the temperature of the heart."

_____

_____

_____

**W4-D5** **READ ROMANS 12:17-21.** What do these verses teach you about forgiveness? In what way do they apply to you today?

_____

_____

_____

_____

_____

# ACTION

How could you continue reminding yourself of the decision you made to forgive? Jot some ideas down here, or use your notes pages to sketch your thoughts.

_____

_____

_____

_____

_____

Select a Scripture verse that will best help you keep making the choice to forgive.

_____

_____

_____

_____

_____

_____

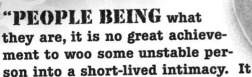

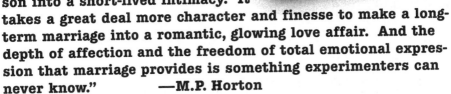

**"PEOPLE BEING** what they are, it is no great achievement to woo some unstable person into a short-lived intimacy. It takes a great deal more character and finesse to make a long-term marriage into a romantic, glowing love affair. And the depth of affection and the freedom of total emotional expression that marriage provides is something experimenters can never know."  **—M.P. Horton**

**"LET YOUR RELIGION** be less of a theory and more of a love affair."  **—G.K. Chesterton**

**YOUR RISE UP EXPERIENCE HIT** a lot of sensitive life issues. But Session Five *really* got personal. It confronted you about your romantic relationships and sexual purity. You came face-to-face with the reality that romance which steps over God's boundaries causes deep, lasting damage.

You also had time to deal with some **GENDER-SPECIFIC** issues. The ladies talked about how the way they dress and act communicates one of two things: either they're a daughter of the King of kings, or they're for sale. The guys faced up to some character issues: how they look at and treat women. They learned a new definition of what it means to be a man.

As if all of that wasn't enough, this session went one step further. It gave you the opportunity to cut unhealthy soul ties with people of the opposite sex.

It can be very difficult to stick to new habits in this area of your life, especially when you get back to school and see your peers doing things you used to do and perhaps still desire to do. That's why you're revisiting Session Five—to "check in" and renew the commitments you made to think and act in ways that are sexually pure—**AND HONORING TO GOD.**

**MEMORIZE . . .**

But store up for yourselves treasures in heaven, where moth and rust do not destroy, and where thieves do not break in and steal. For where your treasure is, there your heart will be also.

—Matthew 6:20-21

**MAKE THESE VERSES** a part of who you are this week.

**WRITE THESE VERSES DOWN,** say them to your little brother over and over again, tape them to your forehead (well, maybe not). Do whatever works best for you!

# WEEK FIVE DAY ONE: CRUSHING THE NUMBERS

**THE FIRST THING** you were confronted with in Session Five was a series of statistics. Your training manual listed some pretty sobering facts about sexual activity that's taking place among your peers—and the price they're paying for it. Here are a few of those numbers again:

**1.** Almost one million teenage girls get pregnant each year (source: The Alan Guttmacher Institute).

**2.** Every year, three million teens acquire an STD (source: The Alan Guttmacher Institute).

**3.** Studies show that the vast majority of teenagers who pledged to remain virgins until they are married ended up having sex before marriage.

**WE SHOWED YOU THESE FACTS** to give you a wake-up call to the reality that outside of marriage, temporary sexual pleasure produces long-term emotional pain. Today's study will continue challenging you to "crush the numbers," starting with your attitude toward sex. You don't have to become a statistic!

# INSPECTION

What did you think about these facts when they were presented at the *Rise Up* retreat? Were you surprised? Shocked? Or was it not a big deal to you?

_____

_____

_____

_____

_____

**READ 1 CORINTHIANS 6:18–20.** Write down three reasons why God instructs us to remain sexually pure.

_____

_____

_____

_____

_____

_____

# ANALYSIS

According to **REVELATION 21:8** and **22:15,** God puts acts of sexual immorality on the same level as murder. Why do you think Christian teenagers continue to become sexually active when they know the Lord takes purity so seriously?

_____

_____

_____

_____

_____

_____

**READ MATTHEW 5:27–29.** What does this passage indicate about the power of your thought life?

_____

_____

_____

_____

_____

**EPHESIANS 4:22–24 SAYS** that the keys to overcoming impurity and lust are to "be made new in the attitude of your mind" and to "put on the new self, created to be like God in true righteousness and holiness." How do you do this?

_____

_____

_____

_____

_____

_____

# ACTION

Based on your answers to the previous question, ask your accountability helpers to assist you in taking these steps toward developing a godly perspective on sex.

_____

_____

_____

_____

_____

_____

_____

_____

# DATING DISTRACTION

**FOR WHERE YOUR TREASURE IS,** there your
heart will be also. **—Matthew 6:21**

**DURING SESSION FIVE** of *Rise Up* you watched a series
of videos that illustrated what happens to people when they
become obsessed with finding their significance in a boyfriend or
girlfriend. They become "spineless," ineffective Christians; they
neglect their relationship with God and His purposes for them.

When you depend on a **"SIGNIFICANT OTHER"** to make
you feel good about yourself, it's very easy to fall into unhealthy
patterns of behavior that hurt you and the people you date.
Today's study is a reminder that God has better things in mind.

# INSPECTION

Ah ... *Insignificant Others*. These videos may have seemed a little
over the top, but they were pretty accurate. In your dating relationships, how have you actually looked like the "lovebirds" in
these flicks? Fake? Infatuated? Manipulative? Obsessive?

_____

_____

_____

_____

_____

_____

_____

# ANALYSIS

**READ MATTHEW 6:20-21.** Where is your heart these days? What does it mean to "store up for yourselves treasures in heaven"?

_____

_____

_____

If Jesus came to you in person today to tell you how He feels about your dating relationships, what do you (honestly) think He would say?

_____

_____

_____

_____

# ACTION

**PROVERBS 4:23 SAYS:** "Above all else, guard your heart, for it is the wellspring of life." What is the most effective thing you can do to guard your heart in regard to dating?

_____

_____

_____

_____

In the notes page of this week's study, draw a simple picture expressing where your heart has been—and where it needs to be in order to honor God.

_____

_____

_____

_____

# SOUL TIES

## KEEP YOURSELF PURE. —1 Timothy 5:22

**TODAY WE'RE LOOKING** at soul ties again. You learned during *Rise Up* that you can develop soul ties *without* physical involvement—*and* that physical involvement *always* creates this bond. Remember the half-eaten candy bar? This game may have seemed pretty funny until you realized what it meant: that the choices you make in the moment have long-term consequences.

**AS YOU LEARNED** during basic training, when you give yourself away sexually, you form a deep connection with that person whether you're willing to acknowledge it or not. And if you don't sever that "soul tie," not only will you not be able to give all of yourself to your spouse someday, you won't be able to give all of yourself to God right now.

# INSPECTION

What was the first thing (or person) that jumped into your mind when you understood the analogy of the half-eaten candy bar? How have you seen this happen in real life?

_____

_____

_____

_____

_____

_____

_____

**W5-D3** In your training manual you wrote down the name of someone you have an unhealthy bond with. Where is that relationship at now?

_____

_____

_____

_____

_____

_____

_____

# ANALYSIS

**EZEKIEL 11:19 TELLS US** that God wants us to have an undivided heart for Him. How does premarital sexual activity cause our hearts to be divided?

_____

_____

_____

_____

_____

_____

**READ 1 CORINTHIANS 6:16–17.** What does it mean to be united (have soul ties) with the Lord? Why do you think the apostle Paul contrasts this union with becoming united with a prostitute?

_____

_____

_____

_____

_____

_____

What is the most powerful expression of godly care for another person? (See John 15:13.) Read more about this quality in 1 Corinthians 13:4–7. How do your soul ties demonstrate these characteristics?

W5-D3

_____

_____

_____

_____

_____

_____

# ACTION

Name three things you need to change in your relationships to make them reflect the kinds of healthy soul ties God intended.

_____

_____

_____

_____

_____

_____

_____

_____

_____

_____

_____

# NOT FOR SALE

## TREAT YOUNGER MEN AS BROTHERS . . . and younger women as sisters, with absolute purity.
### —1 Timothy 5:1–2

**THE NEXT SEGMENT** of Session Five got even more in-your-face about how you interact with the opposite sex. This gender-separated time focused not only on what you do, but why you do these things.

**THE GALS TALKED ABOUT** their clothing choices and flirtation. The guys talked about their mental attitudes and actions toward women. Let's take another look at what men and women of God look and act like.

# INSPECTION

## TO THE GIRLS:
At this point in Session Five, you wrote down the items of clothing you bought for the wrong reasons. Have you gotten rid of them?

_____

_____

You also acknowledged behaviors that tell guys you are for sale—an easy target for sexual gratification. What have you been doing to change these habits?

_____

_____

_____

## TO THE GUYS:

At this point in Session Five, you took time to admit wrong attitudes regarding what it means to be a man, and wrote down what thoughts and behaviors are dishonoring to women and to the Lord. Which of these have you changed since then?

_____

_____

_____

_____

# ANALYSIS

## GIRLS:

In Ruth 3:10, why does Boaz praise Ruth? What does this tell you about what kind of behavior a godly woman should be noted for?

_____

_____

_____

_____

_____

_____

## GUYS:

In Genesis 29:20–21, Jacob worked for seven years to be able to marry the woman he loved—and didn't have sex with her until that time had passed and they had wed. How does this challenge your standards of sexual purity?

_____

_____

_____

_____

**W5-D4**

## BOTH:
If a non-Christian saw you interacting with people of the opposite sex, how would they know you are a believer?

_____

_____

_____

_____

## GIRLS:
Read 1 Timothy 2:9–10. What is Paul's point about modesty?

_____

_____

_____

_____

## GUYS:
Read Matthew 5:28. Where is your brain's purity level today?

_____

_____

_____

_____

# ACTION

**1 TIMOTHY 4:12** tells us to set an example for other believers through our speech, life, love, faith, and purity. How can you set a a better example for your Christian _and_ non-Christian friends?

_____

_____

_____

_____

**WAIT FOR THE LORD;** be strong and take heart and wait for the LORD.

**Psalm 27:14**

**BY THIS TIME IN SESSION FIVE** of *Rise Up,* you probably were feeling hammered by the no-nonsense messages urging you toward higher standards of sexual and relational purity. But you weren't off the hook yet. Now was the time to bring your issues to the altar—and take a leap of faith in this area of your life. You had an opportunity to write your sins in the sand, and wipe them away. Then—you had a chance to "crush the crush." What's been happening since then?

# INSPECTION

After you wiped away the sins you described in the sand, you wrote them out in your training manual. What did you decide to leave behind?

_____

_____

_____

_____

_____

_____

_____

**W5-D5** Have you left behind both those choices *and* the guilt? Remember, what did Jesus say to the adulterous woman in John 8:10–11?

_____

_____

_____

_____

# ANALYSIS

Choosing to "crush the crush" and focus only on God for a year was a major decision. If you took this step, write down what it has required you to do and what that has been like (use your Notes Pages if you need more space). If you didn't choose that route, write down why not and what you think it would take for you to reach that point.

_____

_____

_____

_____

_____

_____

Whether you have chosen to stop dating or to continue to date, God promises in Philippians 4:19 to meet all of your needs (this includes the emotional ones). To what degree do you believe this promise? To what extent are you willing to wait on His timing in this part of your life?

_____

_____

_____

_____

_____

_____

**READ 1 CORINTHIANS 7:32–35.** How can you apply these verses to your decision not to date?

_____

_____

_____

# ACTION

## MEMORIZE THE FOLLOWING VERSE:

> Teach me your way, O LORD,
> and I will walk in your truth;
> give me an undivided heart,
> that I may fear your name.
> **—Psalm 86:11**

Use whatever memorizing method works best for you. But here are some ideas to get you started:

## WRITE THE VERSE OUT SEVERAL TIMES.

**DRAW A PICTURE** of what you think it means (use the extra pages at the end of the week for space).

**SAY IT ALOUD** to a friend, a parent, or even to the mirror. Tape it up wherever you are likely to see it: on the ceiling above your bed, in your locker, or on the fridge door.

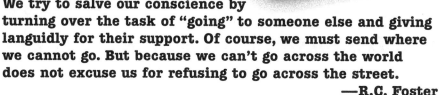

**JESUS SAID,** "Go," but the church through selfishness and indifference has refused to obey. We try to substitute "write," "send," or "give" for "go." We try to salve our conscience by turning over the task of "going" to someone else and giving languidly for their support. Of course, we must send where we cannot go. But because we can't go across the world does not excuse us for refusing to go across the street.

—R.C. Foster

**THE SIXTH SESSION** of the *Rise Up* experience presented a formidable challenge to you: stop gazing at your navel and start saving souls. You heard some grim statistics that summarize a bit of what you probably are already witnessing at school—that your generation is dying, that most teens are buying into the lies of the world . . . and that they're crying out for help.

Who better to help guide them to the light of Jesus Christ than their peers? **WHO BETTER THAN YOU?**

As you choked on that idea, you got a **CLEAR REMINDER** that when you became a Christian, you didn't join a social club. You joined God's army. And as a soldier of the King of kings, you have a specific assignment that nobody but you can carry out for Him. You have a purpose.

Part of that purpose, you realized, could mean serving your Commander not just in America but in other countries. He may want you to go on a short-term mission trip, to **OPEN YOUR EYES** to His **"BIG PICTURE"** and ultimate long-term plan.

This was it—an opportunity for you to step outside of yourself and extend the love of Christ in very tangible ways to people who are walking in spiritual darkness. Were you ready to let His light shine through you at that point? **ARE YOU READY NOW?**

**MEMORIZE . . .**

But in your hearts set apart Christ as Lord. Always be prepared to give an answer to everyone who asks you to give the reason for the hope that you have. But do this with gentleness and respect . . . .

—1 Peter 3:15

**MAKE IT A POINT** to meditate on this verse every day this week.

**COMMIT THESE WORDS** to your heart and mind. Make them a part of your life.

**YOU DID NOT CHOOSE ME,** but I chose you and appointed you to go and bear fruit—fruit that will last.

—John 15:16

**IN THE INTRODUCTION** to Session Six, you heard—perhaps for the first time—that God called you to Himself for two specific reasons: to experience His love, and to share that love with others through the gifts He has given you.

**YOU MAY HAVE THOUGHT** before this moment that you had nothing worthwhile to offer even your next-door neighbor, let alone someone living on the other side of the ocean. Let's take another look at what God says about this—and about you.

# INSPECTION

**ACCORDING TO JEREMIAH 29:11,** what does God say about His plans for your life?

_____

_____

_____

_____

What else does the Bible say about God's plans? (See Psalm 33:11.)

_____

_____

_____

_____

# ANALYSIS

Why is it important to understand God's purpose for you as His adopted son or daughter?

_____

_____

_____

**READ PROVERBS 3:5–6.** How can you know what God is directing you to do for Him?

_____

_____

_____

_____

Describe what your sense of purpose was before you came to *Rise Up: Basic Training for Warriors.* Has it changed? If so, how?

_____

_____

_____

_____

_____

# ACTION

**PROVERBS 20:5 SAYS**, "The purposes of a man's heart are deep waters, but a man of understanding draws them out." What steps can you take to begin drawing out, or putting into action, God's purposes for you?

_____

_____

_____

# WEEK SIX DAY TWO: SPIRITUAL COUCH POTATOES

**SUPPOSE A BROTHER OR SISTER** is without clothes and daily food. If one of you says to him, "Go, I wish you well; keep warm and well fed," but does nothing about his physical needs, what good is it? In the same way, faith by itself, if it is not accompanied by action, is dead.

But someone will say, "You have faith, I have deeds." Show me your faith without deeds, and I will show you my faith by what I do.

You believe that there is one God. Good! Even the demons believe that—and shudder.

—James 2:15–19

**ONCE YOU LEARNED** that God made you for a purpose, you needed to assess your priorities. In your training manual you wrote down how you typically spend your time when you're at school. You may not have considered before that, while it's good to be involved in the activities your school offers, the devil can distract you from dedicating those pursuits to God—or suggest to you that it's okay to toss away what little time you have left on video and computer games or trips to the mall.

**REMEMBER THE STATISTICS** you read about your generation—the drug abuse, the cutting, the suicides? Your peers need to hear about Jesus—from *you*. Your Commander is calling you to active duty. You don't have time to let your faith sit on the couch!

# INSPECTION

Describe a time when you knew God was prompting you to share the love of Christ with someone—but you blew it. In contrast, write down a moment when you said "yes" to God. Write down how you felt about those choices.

_____

_____

_____

_____

_____

_____

**READ REVELATION 3:15-16** and **VERSE 19.** What does God say to believers who are "lukewarm"? Why does He say this?

_____

_____

_____

_____

_____

_____

# ANALYSIS

**READ EPHESIANS 5:15-16** and **COLOSSIANS 4:2-6.**
Why is it important to make the most of the opportunities God gives you to minister to hurting people?

_____

_____

_____

_____

**W6-D2**

How do you think the enemy of your soul has been distracting you from following through on putting your faith into practice?

_____

_____

_____

_____

_____

# ACTION

Based on your above answers, choose one of your personal "faith distractions" and write down how you can keep it from messing up your priorities again.

_____

_____

_____

_____

_____

Ask your accountability partner and advisor to help you keep outreach at the top of your list.

**WE HAVE DIFFERENT GIFTS**, according to the grace given us. If a man's gift is prophesying, let him use it in proportion to his faith. If it is serving, let him serve; if it is teaching, let him teach; if it is encouraging, let him encourage; if it is contributing to the needs of others, let him give generously; if it is leadership, let him govern diligently; if it is showing mercy, let him do it cheerfully.
—**Romans 12:6–8**

**YOU ENLISTED IN GOD'S ARMY**—and He has an assignment tailor-made to fit the way He has gifted you. At this point in Session Six, you took a moment to think about what your role in God's army could be—what He created you to do.

# INSPECTION

How has God gifted you to serve Him? Name at least two ways He has used you to reach out to other people.

_____

_____

_____

_____

_____

_____

_____

_____

_____

_____

**W6-D3** What have your friends and family observed about your abilities? (Consistent feedback is a good indicator of spiritual gifts).

_____
_____
_____
_____
_____
_____

# ANALYSIS

**EPHESIANS 5:1-2** describes Jesus' sacrifice for us as a fragrant offering to God—and says we can imitate this by living a life that demonstrates His love. What does your life smell like these days? If it's not too pleasant, what needs to change?

_____
_____
_____
_____
_____
_____

If you could do anything at all for God, what would it be? (Be creative here! God is a big God—He can handle your ideas. And remember, you can write or draw your ideas. Use the blank pages at the end of the week for extra space.)

_____
_____
_____
_____
_____

# ACTION

Write out a personal mission statement based on your awareness of your spiritual gifts and your interests in certain types of
ministry.

_____

_____

_____

_____

_____

_____

_____

_____

_____

Find out how you could begin sharing your gifts at church or at
youth group.

_____

_____

_____

_____

_____

_____

_____

_____

# THE HARVEST FIELD

**THEREFORE GO AND MAKE DISCIPLES** of all nations, baptizing them in the name of the Father and of the Son and of the Holy Spirit, and teaching them to obey everything I have commanded you. And surely I am with you always, to the very end of the age.

—Matthew 28:19–20.

**ONCE YOU HAD AN OPPORTUNITY** to dream about how God could use you in ministry, you got to dream about *where* He could use you in ministry. In small groups you prayed for people around the world, and you prayed that God would move young people to go to those countries and minister the Gospel. The big questions to consider here were: "Will your youth group go on a missions trip? **WHAT ABOUT YOU?"**

# INSPECTION

Your youth group prayed together, asking God if He wanted you all to take a mission trip together this summer. What did you hear from Him? If He said "yes," describe what the preparations are like, and what you think and feel about it. If God said "no," what is He directing your group to do instead? How will you reach out in your community?

_____

_____

_____

_____

_____

_____

Did you sense a *personal* call to do missions this summer or in the future?

_____

_____

_____

What does Jesus promise to do for us as we introduce other people to Him? (See Matthew 28:20 on page 118.)

_____

_____

_____

_____

_____

# ANALYSIS

When the prophet Isaiah saw that God was looking for a missionary to speak truth to a lost people, he said: "Here am I. Send me!" (Isa. 6:8). What level of commitment are you willing to make to serve God through missions right now?

_____

_____

_____

_____

Write down how you would explain God's plan of salvation to someone who doesn't know Jesus—or English.

_____

_____

_____

_____

_____

_____

# W6-D4 ACTION

If you know at this point that you won't be able to go on a short-term mission trip this summer, don't give up on the idea. Fan the flames! Do research on a country that interests you and write down things you can pray for. Then find out what mission opportunities you could be part of in that country in the future!

_____

_____

_____

_____

_____

_____

_____

Name two ways you would like to express your support of people who are currently pursuing missions work.

_____

_____

_____

_____

_____

_____

_____

_____

**FOR THIS REASON** I remind you to fan into flame the gift of God, which is in you through the laying on of my hands. For God did not give us a spirit of timidity, but a spirit of power, of love and of self-discipline. So do not be ashamed to testify about our Lord, or ashamed of me his prisoner. But join with me in suffering for the gospel, by the power of God, who has saved us and called us to a holy life—not because of anything we have done but because of his own purpose and grace.

—2 Timothy 1:6–9

**AT THE END OF SESSION SIX,** you finally had a chance to put all of these thoughts about missions together. In your training manual you wrote everything you sensed God telling you about your role in reaching the world, the people who so desperately need to be reached, and whether God might have you leave the country to do it.

**THIS WAS A SIGNIFICANT MOMENT**—your moment to turn your back on the devil's lies, give your life away, and say to the Lord: "Here am I, send me!"

# INSPECTION

What message in Session Six impacted you the most?

_____

_____

_____

_____

# W6-D5 ANALYSIS

**READ 1 PETER 3:15** (this week's memory verse). How can you prepare yourself as this verse describes, whether you are in another country or in your own neighborhood?

_____
_____
_____
_____
_____
_____

Jesus gave up His life to bring you to God (1 Peter 3:18). To what extent are you willing to sacrifice in order to bring someone else to God, too?

_____
_____
_____
_____
_____
_____

If you feel hesitant to give all of yourself to God, what's holding you back? What would it take for you to surrender your whole life to Him?

_____
_____
_____
_____
_____
_____
_____

# ACTION

Write down some barriers Christians typically face when they decide to do missions. What would you do to overcome those barriers, or help a fellow believer overcome them?

_____

_____

_____

_____

_____

_____

_____

_____

What will you do to take the gifts God has given you and "fan them into flame"? (2 Tim. 1:6).

_____

_____

_____

_____

_____

_____

_____

_____

_____

_____

_____

_____

_____

"**AM I IGNITABLE?** God deliver me from the dread asbestos of 'other things.' Saturate me with the oil of the Spirit that I may be aflame."
—Jim Elliot

At **LAST—YOU REACHED THE FINAL SESSION** of your *Rise Up* experience. By now you may have been feeling like an overcooked strand of spaghetti. But you still couldn't tune out yet—you still had some soul-searching to do.

You heard about the story of the farmer scattering seed and considered what kind of condition your spiritual soil is in. You had to decide whether you were ready to let God really cultivate in you the lessons you learned during *Basic Training for Warriors*.

And **GUT-WRENCHING LESSONS THOSE WERE!** You went through a review of every session, revisiting the key truths presented and how you responded (or didn't respond).

This study was written to once again remind you of those truths and the commitments you made to live your life fully for God as a soldier in His army. As you begin this final week of Bible study and journaling, let the Lord take you to the next level in your relationship with Him. Let Him take these lessons deeper into your mind and heart and soul. Make the choice to keep following Him—no matter what. **LET HIM SET YOUR FAITH ON FIRE!**

## MEMORIZE . . .

Set your minds on things above, not on earthly things. For you died, and your life is now hidden with Christ in God. When Christ, who is your life, appears, then you also will appear with him in glory.

—Colossians 3:2-4

**AS YOU CEMENT** these words into your mind this week, make it a point to do as it says. Have Jesus on your mind!

**EVEN AFTER YOU** are finished with your *Extreme Commitment* experience, keep reading God's Word daily. Remember, anytime you need a little refresher (for your heart or mind), glance back at your weekly memory verses.

**AND I PRAY THAT YOU**, being rooted and established in love, may have power, together with all the saints, to grasp how wide and long and high and deep is the love of Christ, and to know this love that surpasses knowledge—that you may be filled to the measure of all the fullness of God.

**Ephesians 3:17–19**

**AT THE BEGINNING** of the final session of the *Rise Up* experience, you talked about roots. Deep spiritual roots—the kind that keep your faith strong and enduring long after the spiritual high of a retreat weekend or youth event fades away. You learned that the only way to grow deep roots is to invest time in your relationship with God—and live out your faith. How has that been going?

# INSPECTION

Describe how you typically connect with God. How often do you meet with Him? What do you talk about, and how long do those conversations last? What are you reading in His Word?

_____

_____

_____

_____

_____

_____

_____

_____

**READ MARK 1:35, MATTHEW 14:23, AND LUKE 22:39–46.** Write several characteristics of the time Jesus spent with God.

_____

_____

_____

_____

_____

_____

W7-D1

# ANALYSIS

When you promise to do something, how's your follow-through? Do you make impulsive decisions and forget about them or dismiss them? Or do you make sure to do what you say you're going to do?

_____

_____

_____

_____

_____

_____

**ACCORDING TO JAMES 1:2–4,** why is perseverance an important part of our faith? How does this apply to your relationship with God?

_____

_____

_____

_____

_____

**W7-D1** Where does time in God's Word land on your priority list . . . and why? Read the following descriptions of God's Word. How do these affect your perspective?

## HEBREWS 4:12
## PSALM 12:6
## PSALM 119:103–105, 130, 133
## JEREMIAH 23:29

_____

_____

_____

_____

_____

_____

_____

# ACTION

Make a commitment to spend time with God. Decide how often and for how long, and ask your accountability helpers to keep you on track. Keep in mind that it takes about 30 days to develop a habit, so stick with it!

_____

_____

_____

_____

_____

_____

_____

# A GLANCE AT THE MIRROR

## WEEK SEVEN DAY TWO.

**DO NOT MERELY LISTEN** to the word, and so deceive yourselves. Do what it says. Anyone who listens to the word but does not do what it says is like a man who looks at his face in the mirror and, after looking at himself, goes away and immediately forgets what he looks like. But the man who looks intently into the perfect law that gives freedom, and continues to do this, not forgetting what he has heard, but doing it—he will be blessed in what he does.

—**James 1:22–25**

**WHY DO YOU STUDY** for exams at school? So you can review the lessons you have learned in order to pass your tests. In the same way, during Session Seven of *Rise Up* your youth group leader walked you through a review of the six key ways a committed faith changes the way you live:

▶ **IT CAUSES** you to turn and run from your sin nature.

▶ **IT SEES THROUGH** the lies of the media.

▶ **IT REVOLUTIONIZES** how you see yourself and your relationship with God.

▶ **IT CHANGES** how you interact with your family.

▶ **IT TRANSFORMS** your view of the opposite sex.

▶ **IT MAKES YOU THINK** about the friends you let into your life.

**FOR TODAY'S STUDY,** write down what each of these areas of your life looked like before the *Rise Up* retreat, how you see them changing, and where God is telling you they need to be. Include for each area a Bible verse that's helping you get there.

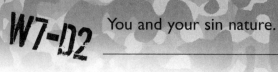

You and your sin nature.

_____

_____

_____

You and the media.

_____

_____

_____

_____

You and God.

_____

_____

_____

_____

You and your family.

_____

_____

_____

_____

You and the opposite sex.

_____

_____

_____

_____

You and your friends.

_____

_____

_____

_____

# LIVING FOR GOD

**SINCE, THEN, YOU HAVE BEEN RAISED** with Christ, set your hearts on things above, where Christ is seated at the right hand of God. Set your minds on things above, not on earthly things. For you died, and your life is now hidden with Christ in God. When Christ, who is your life, appears, then you will also appear with him in glory.

Put to death, therefore, whatever belongs to your earthly nature: sexual immorality, impurity, lust, evil desires and greed, which is idolatry. Because of these, the wrath of God is coming. **—Colossians 3:1–6**

**YOUR TRAINING MANUAL** contained seven statements that describe the life of a person who lives for God. These statements were the elements of an oath of allegiance—an opportunity for you to make a significant commitment to God. Here are those statements again:

▶ **I WILL REMEMBER** what Jesus did for me and that He deserves my all.

▶ **I WILL FIND MY VALUE** in who God says I am. I'm worth His Son dying for me.

▶ **I WILL MEDITATE** on God's Word in areas where I have been weak so that when I'm tempted again, I will over come. I refuse to be a slave to sin any longer.

▶ **MY BEST FRIENDS** will be those who love God with all of their hearts. Others must be acquaintances. I will honor my father and mother.

▶ **I WILL GUARD** my heart and focus on God, not a guy or girl.

▶ **I WILL BE A DISCIPLE** of Jesus, always learning and growing.

▶ **I WILL MAKE MY LIFE** count to reach this generation and the world!

# W7-D3 INSPECTION

What does the apostle Paul instruct Christians to do in Ephesians 4:1?

_____

_____

_____

_____

_____

_____

Summarize Jesus' example of a God-centered life in Philippians 2:1–8.

_____

_____

_____

_____

_____

_____

# ANALYSIS

## READ DEUTERONOMY 30:20 and COLOSSIANS 3:4. What does the statement "the LORD is your life" mean to you?

_____

_____

_____

_____

_____

_____

Write an example of how you are living for God in each of the seven areas listed at the beginning of this lesson.

_____

_____

_____

_____

_____

_____

_____

_____

_____

_____

**IN 1 THESSALONIANS 4:1,** Christians are urged to "live in order to please God" more and more. Why?

_____

_____

_____

# ACTION

Just before Joshua (the leader of the Israelites) died, he challenged them: "Choose for yourselves this day whom you will serve. . . . But as for me and my house, we will serve the LORD" (Josh. 24:15). How will you make this choice in your own life? What will it look like?

_____

_____

_____

_____

_____

_____

_____

# FOLLOWING JESUS

**ANYONE WHO DOES NOT CARRY** his cross and follow me cannot be my disciple.

**Jesus – Luke 14:27**

**AS YOU CAME CLOSE** to finishing your *Rise Up* experience, you looked at all the things you said you were going to do when you got home. At this time, your youth group leader gave you another gut check. Were you really committing to give your life fully to God, or were you just caught up in the moment? Were you ready to demonstrate the lifestyle of a disciple—**A TRUE CHRIST-FOLLOWER?**

# INSPECTION

How did King Solomon make God angry in 1 Kings 11:6?

_____

_____

What does Jesus promise to people who follow Him in John 8:12?

_____

_____

# ANALYSIS

In the Great Commission (Matt. 28:19–20), Jesus doesn't tell us to go and make Christians of all nations. He tells us to make *disciples* of all nations. Why does He say this? What's the difference?

_____

_____

Are you a Christian in name only, or are you a disciple of Jesus?

_____

_____

_____

Jesus defines the proof that someone is truly His disciple in John 8:31–32. How does your answer to the previous question line up with this proof?

_____

_____

_____

What is Jesus saying to you right now about being His disciple?

_____

_____

_____

# ACTION

When the going got tough for Jesus in Matthew 26:56, *all* of his disciples deserted Him and ran away. Decide right now how you are going to respond when things get tough for you. Will you stand by the Lord through all of your difficulties? Or will you abandon your Christian faith?

_____

_____

_____

_____

# LIVING THE OATH

**HOW MUCH MORE, THEN,** will the blood of Christ, who through the eternal Spirit offered himself unblemished to God, cleanse our consciences from acts that lead to death, so that we may serve the living God!

Hebrews 9:14

**BUT BE SURE TO FEAR THE LORD** and serve him faithfully with all your heart; consider what great things he has done for you.

1 Samuel 12:24

**THIS WAS IT**—the last few moments of the *Rise Up* experience. You had some time to write in your training manual what you were thinking and feeling, and to remind yourself of the key lessons you had learned throughout basic training. Then you decided whether you were ready to sign the "Oath of Allegiance" to God. Signing it indicated a significant commitment on your part and was not to be made lightly.

**FOR TODAY'S STUDY,** take some time to write about what the *Rise Up* and *Over the Edge* experiences have meant to you. How have you seen God working in your life through these? Write a prayer expressing your heart to God, thanking Him for specific ways He has touched you and helped you. Tell Him more about your dreams for ministry and ask Him to help you get there. What kind of Christian do you want to be? Are you ready to be a soldier? Are you ready to live the oath?

> Trust in him at all times, O people;
> pour out your hearts to him,
> for God is our refuge.
> —Psalm 62:8

# Introducing
# Acquire the Fire
## Teen Devotional Magazine

**A hot new full-color teen devotional that flips—half for guys and half for girls.**

Exclusively for teens, this is a magazine that will help them discover God's truth and stand firm in today's media-driven culture.

You'll find:

- Each issue structured around five hot teen topics
- 40 biblically-sound Devos in each issue
- Music reviews

- Articles written by teens and youth leaders
- Real-life faith stories
- Quizzes
- Teen-to-Teen Wisdom
- "Top 10" Lists

**Available Quarterly**

**Also Available!**
Companion <u>Discussion Guide</u> for Youth Workers and Parents

# The Word at Work Around the World

A vital part of Cook Communications Ministries is our international outreach, Cook Communications Ministries International (CCMI). Your purchase of this book, and of other books and Christian-growth products from Cook, enables CCMI to provide Bibles and Christian literature to people in more than 150 languages in 65 countries.

Cook Communications Ministries is a not-for-profit, self-supporting organization. Revenues from sales of our books, Bible curricula, and other church and home products not only fund our U.S. ministry, but also fund our CCMI ministry around the world. One hundred percent of donations to CCMI go to our international literature programs.

CCMI reaches out internationally in three ways:

• Our premier International Christian Publishing Institute (ICPI) trains leaders from nationally led publishing houses around the world.

• We provide literature for pastors, evangelists, and Christian workers in their national language.

• We reach people at risk—refugees, AIDS victims, street children, and famine victims—with God's Word.

## Word Power, God's Power

Faith Kidz, RiverOak, Honor, Life Journey, Victor, NexGen — every time you purchase a book produced by Cook Communications Ministries, you not only meet a vital personal need in your life or in the life of someone you love, but you're also a part of ministering to José in Colombia, Humberto in Chile, Gousa in India, or Lidiane in Brazil. You help make it possible for a pastor in China, a child in Peru, or a mother in West Africa to enjoy a life-changing book. And because you helped, children and adults around the world are learning God's Word and walking in his ways.

Thank you for your partnership in helping to disciple the world. May God bless you with the power of his Word in your life.

*For more information about our international ministries, visit www.ccmi.org.*